THE MARKETPLACE GUIDE TO

VICTORIAN FURNITURE

THE MARKETPLACE GUIDE TO

VICTORIAN FURNITURE

Styles & Values

PETER S. BLUNDELL

PHIL T. DUNNING

Designed and Produced by
CATHERINE THURO

THE MARKETPLACE GUIDE TO
VICTORIAN FURNITURE
Styles & Values

ISBN 0-89145-166-8

Additional copies of this book may be ordered from:

Collector Books,   OR   Thorncliffe House Inc.
Box 3009,   4 William Morgan Dr., Thorncliffe Park,
Paducah, Kentucky 42001   Toronto, Ontario M4H 1E6

$17.95   ($19.95 in Canada)
Add $1.00 for Postage and Handling.

Designed and Produced by Catherine Thuro
Staff Artist, John R. Wright
Typeset in Souvenir Light by Canada Stamp
Color separations by Colour Separations of Canada Ltd.
Printed and bound in Canada by The Bryant Press Ltd.

Published simultaneously in Canada by Thorncliffe House Inc.

Published by

Collector Books
Box 3009
Paducah, Kentucky 42001

To Carl

Introduction

This book is intended as a practical collector's guide to the variety of furniture made in the Victorian era that is on the market today. All the pieces illustrated were for sale at the time they were photographed. They vary in quality from great to mediocre; from pristine original finishes to heavily stripped examples. The range is intentional, to give you a feel for what is available. There are a number of similar examples of some forms for comparison of details, design, price range, etc. Major characteristics of the styles popular during Victoria's reign are set out in a separate section. The examples photographed show "variations on a theme". There is also a glossary and a "who's who" of important names in furniture at the time.

The Marketplace Guide does not intend to be the final word in the field; it addresses particular questions. The bibliography lists a number of publications, including reprints of "primary source material" — books and catalogs of the period. These not only give the most accurate idea of the Victorian approach to decoration and furniture, but are fascinating reading.

In producing a book from "in the field" specimens, there are limiting factors of time and availability in photographing, examining, and recording pieces. Please keep this in mind. Occasionally, measurements were not available. More important, woods described are on visual analysis only — and that is at best an uncertain method. Age, dirt and possibly an original attempt to fool the eye by the maker all confuse positive identification. If, for some reason it is deemed necessary, microcellular examination of a sample is the only conclusive process.

Construction methods as a means of dating furniture have not been discussed here, although useful references are included in the bibliography. Learning to judge a piece by design or style, construction methods, and signs of age are part of any collector's education: read, look. Pick books from the bibliography, go to museums and shops. Above all, ask questions. Become comfortable with *your* assessment of a piece, not just what is told to you. Finally, and most important, enjoy the process. As one who has been "hooked" for many years, I hope you derive as much pleasure as I have from learning and buying.

Phil T. Dunning

Acknowledgements

By Peter S. Blundell

My search for furniture took me to many parts of the United States and Canada. Most of the people I met recognized the need for books of this nature, and gave me an endless amount of encouragement. Without their help and patience this book could never have emerged as it has from the rough-and-tumble of the marketplace.

I would like to thank all of the following who assisted me in the preparation of this book.

My wife Marian, who took complete charge of our antique store as well as coping with our two small children.

Catherine and Carl Thuro for their expertise with books and all their guidance.

Phil Dunning who wrote the text. We spent many hours viewing slides and discussing both the furniture and the marketplace. His curatorial expertise is apparent in the interesting information he presents.

Thomas Blundell, my father for his encouragement and help.

My father-in-law Dr. E. C. Webster, for his support over the years.

Penny Savosh who helped us amazingly and consistently for "the fun of it" — a special vote of thanks.

The Reid Girls Flea Market at Brimfield, Massachusetts, who allowed our mobile studio to clutter up the sales field for three days and organized work teams for us, and lots more.

My thanks to Jill Reid Lukesh and Judith Reid Mathieu of "Antique Acres" I wish them continued success.

Fred Dole of the Reid Girls Flea Market who lent us equipment when ours failed in the heat, and who gave us much good advice.

George J. Silverman of Lawrence Massachusetts for his kindness and precious time. Also John and Mary Silverman for their consideration, company and hospitality.

And also to:
Betty Adam
Patricia & Jim Alex
Howard J. Arkush
Jim & Theresa Barker
Molly Bartram
Sergio Bernardi
James Bisback
Michael Bucino
Betty Bull
Russell Carrell
The Cavanagh Group
Ken Chapman
Doris & Pete Clements
Cy Cline
Phyllis Detour
Brian Dodge

John Espeland
Irene & Robert Faubert
Royal F. Feltner
John Garreau
Zella & Vic Goetz
Stephen Goetz
Brenda Gray
Tony Greist
Marion Hagey
The Halversons
The Hetheringtons
Linda Howard
Bill Hawkes
Finella Hughes
Jonny H. P. Kalisch
Tom Keeling
June Kennedy
Jeanne Kesten
Donna Kay & Jerry Keyer
Verla Leach
Steve Lee
Bob & Ray Long
Leslie Losonczki
Joe MacDougall
Carol & Dick Morse

Gene Ploss
'Red' & 'Bum' Porter
Mona Pettigrew
The Rays
Ken & Lori Rifenburg
Gay Robertson
Ralph Rosetti
The Sharkeys
Herman Steckerl
Henry Stevenson
David Stewart
Mary Sutherland
The Swainsons
Jack Truesdale
Tom Valentino
Champ & Bob Watson
Robert Watts
Wimodausis Club
Ron Windebank
Betty Wolf
'Antique Andy' Worrell
Paul Zammitt

The Marketplace - Past

The Victorian Era saw a major revolution both in furniture production and marketing. When Victoria ascended to the throne in 1837, the individual cabinetmaker in his shop, perhaps with journeymen and apprentices, held sway in the field. The shop itself, and the tools in it, had not changed markedly in generations. The only source of power to turn the lathe and work the saw came from those who labored there, or at best from a water wheel.

The cabinetmaker often took on tasks in a number of related fields, from house building to undertaking, since it was he who built and delivered the coffin.

If a customer desired a piece of furniture, he went directly to the craftsman. Most had some standard items in stock — tables, beds, etc. — but if that customer wanted something a bit different, he sat down and talked it over with the cabinetmaker. A design was agreed upon, a bargain struck and, in due course, the piece was produced.

Even as the era began, this age-old arrangement was starting to change, and by the end it was only a memory to most people. The forces that brought about such a change were numerous: new sources of power, better transportation, a larger population, even more wide-spread literacy.

The 1830's and '40's saw the introduction of many improved and labor-saving devices into the workshop. An aspiring cabinetmaker, writing home to his father in Scotland, describes some of the machinery to be found in a North American factory in 1845: ". . . . they have a steam engine and circular saws in full operation, 4 or 5 turning lathes, ... frames with sliding apparatus that square up their wood to any size and require no planing . . . ." The young woodworker had noted, as well as the machines, another important innovation: steam power. These two factors encouraged the division of labor, the final step towards mass production. Workers would no longer be cabinetmakers, but would become carvers, finishers, etc.

The traditional cabinetmaker was thus presented with a challenge. He could, if economics allowed, bring machines into his shop, purchase pre-made parts to speed production and, for a few, develop his own business into a factory. For many, however, the task was too great, and competition with mass production proved impossible.

For the customer, the new techniques meant changes as well. "Machine-made" held no stigma then. It symbolized progress, invention and low prices. Furniture "warerooms" sprang up in larger centres, and the direct connection between producer and consumer disappeared. A new affluence meant that shoppers in these warerooms might consider purchasing a matching parlor or bedroom suite, rather than acquiring individual pieces, as was usual previously. The latest styles were no longer advertised, or "puffed" as they said, as "well-made" or "useful", but as "elegant" and "new". Decoration and carving, now that machinery had made them inexpensive, were the prime consideration for much of the period. For the first time too, the customer could look to the printed word to be told what the fashion was, and what was suitable for his home. Books such as A. J. Downing's *The Architecture of Country Houses* (1850), and Charles Locke Eastlake's, *Hints on Household Taste* (1868), were full of furniture illustrations and decorating ideas. As well, magazines like *Harper's Weekly* and *Godey's Lady's Book* regularly devoted space to interior decorating. All these were avidly read and followed.

As the era went on, there was some backlash against the machine-made *look* of the mid-century, but the factory itself continued to grow. By the 1890's, the average person not only read about the latest styles in books, but purchased them from books as well. The huge mail-order houses — Montgomery Ward, Sears, Roebuck and Eaton's in Canada — had appeared, and the age of the cabinet shop had come to an end.

The Marketplace - Present

We live in an age of nostalgia for a "simpler" life and a more stable world. For many, this is personified by Queen Victoria and her era. Coupled with a strong lean towards the eclectic in interior design today, it has created a flourishing market in Victoriana. There is, in fact, a definite resemblance between the modern collector's taste for diversity and the marketplace in the later Victorian years. Few people want the massive clutter we associate with those times, but a mixture of interesting and heterogeneous furnishings *is* appealing. Stimulating this trend is the growing enthusiasm for renovating and restoring Victorian homes. Furniture of the period complements the detail and character seen in even modest dwellings. This interest has been growing steadily over the last thirty or so years. When Thomas Ormsbee published his landmark, *Field Guide to American Victorian Furniture* in 1952, many people, including dealers, were puzzled or amused by his interest in the period. Today, those same people are buying and selling Victoriana. Realization that much of this furniture is well designed and built has overcome a prejudice which dates from the 1920's and '30's. Then, when collecting "Early American" was high fashion, Victoria's death was within memory of most serious collectors.

Although "great" pieces of Victorian furniture do come on the market today, they are becoming scarce and are snapped up quickly. However, there is a sizable quantity of good-to-fine examples to be found in most shops, shows and flea markets. Availability does vary somewhat across the country. As more interest is generated in the Midwest and West, an unseen army of pickers, wholesalers and haulers move tractor-trailers from the Eastern Seaboard to dealers who can purchase on a large scale. Also growing in scale is the interest in Victoriana in Common Market countries, especially Great Britain. Buyers from Europe are appearing in North America to take back stock for a burgeoning market. All this contributes to a price structure which can do nothing but rise, and the individual can feel secure in investing time and money.

As in any field of collecting, the collector should develop a background so that he feels comfortable in making decisions from his own knowledge. As well, it is extremely useful to locate those dealers who specialize in Victorian furniture and develop a relationship with them.

This will ensure that you will at least be called when a particularly good piece comes in, and you must make the effort to see and assess that piece and make a decision quickly. Even if you do not buy it, your attitude indicates to the dealer that you are serious, and he will make the effort himself to phone again next time.

Finally, and from personal experience, I cannot say too strongly: if you see a piece which you like, which you feel is reasonably priced, which fits your standards and limits of collecting, buy it. If you do not, the chances are it will not remain unsold long, and the next time you see it — if there is a next time — you may be assured it will not be as attractively priced as previously. All collectors have a handful of "I could kick myself for passing up . . . ." stories. I hope yours will not be as plentiful as mine.

Glossary

Acanthus — Conventionalized leaf ornament derived from classical Greek and Roman decoration.

Anthemion — Conventionalized Greek fan-shaped leaf motif, sometimes used interchangeably with *Palmette*.

Bead, Beading — A small, semi-circular molding.

Boss — A raised, rounded ornament, often applied.

Cabochon — An oval, rounded convex ornament, derived from similarly-cut gemstones.

Cabriole — A leg curving outward at the knee and inward at the ankle, forming an S-curve.

Cartouche — Ornamental panel in various forms — sometimes carved, sometimes applied. May be in the form of an unrolled scroll or an elongated, flattened oval.

Cyma curve — A double or S-curve; an *Ogee* curve.

Drop (pendant) — Hanging ornament, usually turned and hanging free, or half round and applied. Opposite of *Finial*.

Finger Molding — Incised, half-round continuous groove on exposed wood frames. Sometimes called thumb molding.

Finial — A decorative terminal, projecting upward, usually fully turned or applied and half round.

Fretwork — Interlaced ornamental work (lattice-work) either pierced or carved in low relief.

Incised — Carving cut into a surface, as opposed to raised from it.

Klysmos — The classic Greek chair supported on four out-curving sabre legs with simple curved back and crestrail.

Ogee — A double or S-curve (see Cyma curve).

Palmette — A fan or palm-shaped motif (see Anthemion).

Pediment — The triangular or rounded top on bookcases, beds, etc. Derived from the gable above the portico of a classical temple. A broken pediment has a central gap before the apex, often with an ornament therein.

Pompeiian leg — A slim, turned leg with a large flattened bun element at the top.

Quatrefoil — A four-lobed ornament resembling a four-leafed clover.

Roundel — Any ornamental disk.

Sabre leg — A C-curved leg resembling the shape of a cavalry sword.

Survival — Term applied to pieces made in a style generally outdated by the time of their manufacture: conservative in design and very old-fashioned. Not to be confused with later stylistic revivals or reproductions.

Swag — A decoration representing drapery hung from two points; also, a pendant ornament, usually carved, representing clusters of fruit and foliage, etc.

Transitional — Having elements of two styles combined in one piece; an older more conservative style and a newer, innovative style.

Trefoil — A three-lobed ornament resembling a three-leafed clover.

Contents

A spectacular bed! This Renaissance ▷
high-back bed features a well-conceived
combination of color, carving and woods.
The base wood is walnut and the raised
panels are burled-walnut veneer. Various
hand-carved motifs culminate in an
imposing central cartouche with pendant
fruit-and-leaf swag. Late 1850's - 1870's.
h. 99", w. 62".

a.

b.

(b) Another Victorian Renaissance bed with characteristics that are avidly sought-after in today's marketplace. The light-toned veneered raised ornaments on the headboard contrast with the darker finish of the walnut base wood. Stiles, or upright supports are topped with turned winged finials that resemble a trophy cup. The elaborate trim also includes curved molding, incised decoration and typically Renaissance elongated oval cartouches. This bed matches the washstand on page 29. h. 89", w. 61".

(a) Architectural elements belie the smaller proportions of this bed. The headboard, with an ornate pediment and applied panels recalls a Renaissance portal. Bosses and mushroom-capped finials are included in the applied trim. The selection and placement of the burled-walnut veneer is striking. The base wood is walnut. h. 85", w. 52".

Pure Victorian Renaissance styling in walnut. Graceful lines are embellished with carving that includes applied roundels, a central cartouche and palmettes, all of which have incised detailing. The finials are finely turned. h. 92", w. 60".

a.

(a) Linear design and incised carving are characteristics of the Eastlake style. This cherrywood bed has raised panels that feature contrasting shades of the heartwood. 1870's - 1880's. h. 76", w. 57".

(b) Another bed with Eastlake elements. Contrasting wood is used for all the applied trim. Flat rather than turned finials have round bosses that are repeated at the top of the headboard. This bed matches the dresser on page 43. h. 75", w. 57".

(c) A massive Victorian Renaissance bed with little surface area that has escaped some form of trim. The three oval moldings on the headboard are unusually placed in the vertical, rather than horizontal. There is a composition molded female face on the pediment. h. 89", w. 62".

b.

c.

All beds on this page would be classed as Victorian cottage furniture.

(a) Graceful curves outline this simple well-proportioned pine bed. Bedroom furniture of this type was originally painted with false graining and flowers similar to the example on page 42b. If the original painted finish became worn or marred it was customary to overpaint the piece. Following this the trend has been to remove all trace of paint to expose the base wood. 1860's - 1880's. h. 56", w. 56".

a.

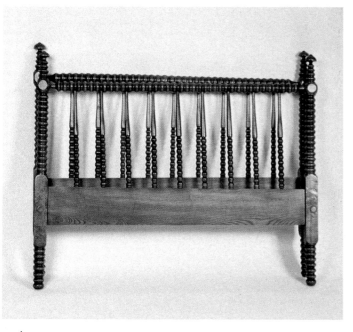

b.

c.

(b) Spool-turned beds were a popular form of mid-Victorian cottage furniture. In Victorian days they were often referred to as Elizabethan. This earlier style has mushroom-cap finials with irregularities in the turnings indicating they were hand produced. h. 44", w. 54".

(c) The more common style of spool-turned bed above was factory made with machined turnings. The term "Jenny Lind" has been given to these beds because of the popularity of the Swedish songstress at the time these beds were in vogue. h. 41", w. 53".

a. Hermon W. Ladd of Chelsea, Massachusetts, obtained an invention patent No. 107509, for this folding bed on Sept. 20, 1870. His name and four prestigious addresses are stencilled on the siderails of this ingenious piece of furniture. Eastlake period cast-iron hardware was used.

The head- and footboards are connected to the legs, and in a single operation they all fold parallel to the siderails. This leaves the bed resting upon the "D" curved frame which permits the bed to be easily rolled on its side. The curved members are then folded in as illustrated in the detail below.

With all parts folded, the bed measures 12" x 39" x 72". The width of the bed was probably dictated by the relationship of the curved rollers to the height. Empire influence has survived in the rolling-pin headboard and footboard.

b.

Detail of folding bed

(b) An "OXFORD JUNIOR FOLDING BED" made by the Welch Folding Bed Co. of Grand Rapids, Michigan, is enclosed in this piece of furniture which was designed to look like a wardrobe. Original simulated-mahogany finish. h. 66".

a.

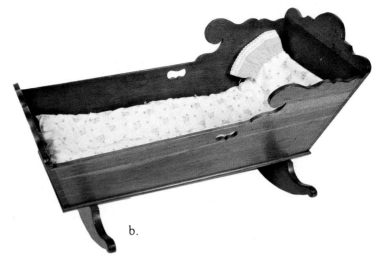

b.

c.

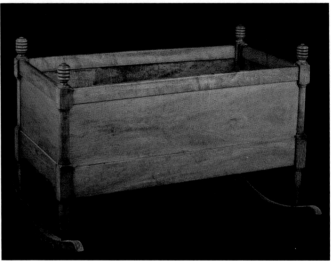

d.

It was customary for most babies to sleep in a rocking cradle of some sort. Handmade and factory-made rocking cradles ranged from crude to finely crafted. They were made for the poor and the wealthy, and often with styling that would relate to other furniture in the household. There were hooded ones that would offer protection from draft or sunlight. Others had solid sides, slats or spindles.

(a) Hand craftsmanship is evident in this rocking cradle. Its most noteable feature is the strength and simplicity of design. h. 21", l. 38", w. 18".

(b) Country Empire influence is apparent in this example with beautiful scalloping and heart-shaped finger grips. It is made in cherry with some heartwood striping, and has good dovetailing at the corners. h. 18", l. 36", w. 17".

(c) A four-post rocking cradle with solid sides and wooden peg construction. This type of cradle was usually painted in a solid color.

(d) This rocking cradle has turned finials and corner posts to relieve its box-like proportions. l. 37", w. 19".

(e) A pine rocking cradle that retains its original finish. Original grained finish commands a higher price in today's marketplace. The shaping at the front of the hood is an attractive detail. h. 26", l. 40" w. 18".

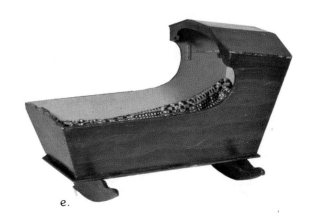

e.

Swinging cradles were popular in the 1890's, and several styles were offered in mail-order catalogs. Rounded or bentwood ends or slats give a curvilinear appearance to the examples shown here. In addition to their original use, today their highly decorative quality has made them in great demand for holding plants.

(a) Mass production of bentwood was engendered by Michael Thonet in the 1850's. It is featured in the ends and legs of the cradle on the right. The spacing of the spindles on the sides and ends is an interesting detail. h. 35", l. 40", w. 18".

a.

(b) Bent slats are suspended from a bentwood frame in this walnut cradle. They resemble ribs of a boat, and the fiddle-head end supports are also similar to those used on boats. Original stencilled detail and traces of light green paint remain. h. 37", l. 46", w. 24".

b.

Victorian Renaissance cottage quality is apparent in this swinging cradle of maple. It was factory made. The bottom cross stretcher is bolted to the ends with the bolts concealed by applied roundels. Mail-order catalogs offered swinging cradles knocked down for shipping. h. 38", l. 41".

a.

(a) This crib or child's bed is a simple form of Eastlake design, probably of the 1880's or 1890's. The headboard is decorated with incised machine carving. h. 42", l. 51", w. 28".

(b) Folding cribs were popular throughout the last quarter of the 19th century. The example illustrated with folding sideguards, was made by the Downing Carriage Co. of Erie, Pennsylvania. It was patented in 1879 and called the "Gem Folding Crib". When the legs were folded under, the small roller casters mounted on the sides of each leg would allow the crib to be pushed under a larger bed, thus becoming a trundle bed.

b.

With little or no plumbing, the washstand was an important part of bedroom furnishings. It held the pitcher and basin, and, from the late 1850's onward, several other matching accessories.

(a) A superb example that embodies the essence of Victorian Renaissance. The fanciful fretwork on the back is continued along the sides. The carving is then re-emphasized on the supports of the towel bar. Circular moldings are applied to the doors, side panels and back. Late 1850's - 1870's. h. 48", w. 48", d. 21".

a.

b.

(b) Crotch-grained mahogany veneer is the most striking feature of this cherry washstand. The style is transitional from Empire to Victorian. Machined beading has been used on the doors and the towel bars have been removed. h. 37", w. 35", d. 18".

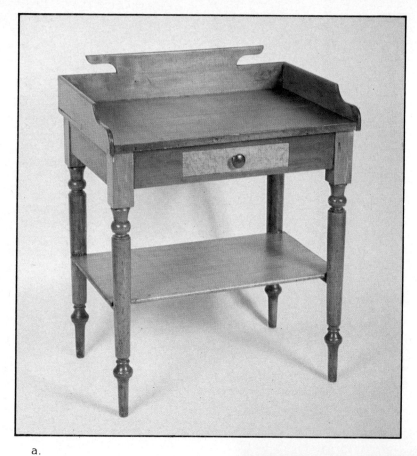

a.

(a) Survival-Sheraton style is evident in a later Victorian washstand. Mixed woods are used with cherry predominant, and a bird's-eye maple drawer. h. 34", w. 28", d. 20".

(b) This washstand is a country piece that also includes several woods. The top is solid bird's-eye maple, and ash is predominant. Molded composition handles simulate hand carving. h. 41", w. 36", d. 17".

b.

The Victorian Renaissance washstand above would have been part of a first-quality bedroom suite. The marble top has corners rounded to match the feet, and lamp brackets only a few inches deep. Walnut is used with figured walnut veneer on raised panels. Drawer trim includes a split cartouche with an applied rosette and carved leaf handles. h. 43", w. 34", d. 17".

a. A whimsical country washstand, predominately pine, from Quebec. h. 43", w. 33", d. 17".

b. This survival Sheraton walnut washstand or server has a particularly fine turned leg. h. 30", w. 36", d. 18".

c. Open elm washstands like the above, with simply-shaped splashboard remained popular into the later 19th century.

d. The "spool" turnings on this walnut piece resemble more closely than usual actual spools strung together.

(a) Scalloped splashboard and base enliven this simple elm washstand. The towel bars and arms are turned, and the pulls are stamped brass with steel bails. 1890's.
h. 36", w. 34", d. 17".

(b) This pine lift-top commode of the 1870's - 90's would formerly have been painted with stencilling and possibly graining.
h. 30", w. 30", d. 18".

(c) An Empire style lift-top commode with crotch-grained mahogany veneer, and flat, scrolled front feet.
h. 31", w. 31", d. 20".

a.

b.

c.

Tables designed to hold toilet accessories are called dressing tables.
A swinging mirror, one or more drawers and a shelf or two were usual.
The obvious plethora of turnings on the example above including
barleytwist turnings, rope turnings and pineapple turnings were
intended to give this late 19th century dressing table an Elizabethan
flavor. Cast-iron ball-and-claw feet. h. 65", w. 38", d. 19".

Some dressing tables had lift tops, some were compartmentalized and others such as the example above had small drawers below the mirror. Its relatively fine lines and turnings suggest an early Empire date, without quite the heaviness of later pieces. A mahogany veneer with pronounced grain has been used. h. 72", w. 42", d. 24".

a.

Some dressers, also called chests of drawers or commodes, were sold as part of a matching bedroom suite, while others were made as individual pieces. In today's market they compare favorably with new furniture in price, and far out-strip new pieces in terms of quality and resale value.

b.

(a) The dresser above is a simple mid-Victorian style. Mirrored application of a crotch-grained mahogany veneer on the three large drawers, and the emphatic flitch apparent on the top drawer are accentuated by the white marble top. The narrow overhanging drawer, uninterrupted by hardware, accommodates concealed finger-grips. The mirror, often referred to today as a wishbone form, also has a mahogany veneered frame. h. 65", w. 46", d. 21".

(b) The application of veneer, in combination with a white marble top, is similar in these two dressers. In this example the drawers are separated by half-round bearer strips. The mirror frame has sinuous lines which seem to portend the languid curves of the later Art Nouveau period.

A large mid-century dresser with bonnet drawers. Many examples of country painted furniture attempt to simulate the bold crotch-grained mahogany veneered treatment on the dresser above. It is supported on four sturdy, turned feet. h. 48", w. 46", d. 22".

a.

The distinctive architectural galleries on the dressers illustrated on these pages have given rise to the term — "chimney-pot" dressers.

(a) The unusual graining in the veneer is the most outstanding feature of this Empire dresser. h. 52", w. 45", d. 21".

(b) An unusual drawer arrangement, with two small drawers above one large drawer, all overhanging a more typical arrangement below. Butternut. h. 56", w. 46", d. 21".

(c) Very similar in design to 36b, but in cherry with heartwood visible on the top edge. h. 59", w. 48", d. 21".

b.

c.

A straightforward country Empire piece in very attractive cherry.
h. 48", w. 44", d. 19".

Tiger-striped maple with a cherry carcass or body. A marvellous example of Empire design with flat-sided scroll feet and an overhanging ogee top drawer. The other drawers including the small ones mounted against the backboard are bordered with applied moldings. 1835-1850. h. 55", w. 47", d. 21".

(a) An impressive solid bird's-eye maple dresser. Full columns, vase turnings and contrasting cherrywood give it a distinctive appearance. Other noteable features of this mid-century Empire piece are the ebonized knobs, diamond-shaped inlaid keyhole escutcheons and half-round bearer strips.
h. 51", w. 50", d. 22".

a.

(b) Survival Empire styling with sweeping scrolled reeded supports. On the top is a recessed case containing two drawers. The overhanging section has two bonnet drawers and two small drawers. The shape of the carved handles has given rise to the term "moustache pulls" and they were generally machine carved or composition molded. Although made and patented earlier they appear most frequently on furniture made during the last quarter of the 19th century.
h. 56", w. 50", d. 22".

b.

(a) The distinctive piece below is an unusual tiered-style five drawer dresser in walnut. The bold design of the backboard is reminiscent of a maple leaf, and the scalloped skirt is applied. This country piece was probably custom made. h. 56", w. 38", d. 18".

a.

b.

(b) Above is a country style dresser in butternut, with machine-carved walnut pulls. The mirror with fretwork supports is somewhat akin to that on page 34b. It is mounted at the back of a recessed lift-top compartment. h. 63", w. 40", d. 19".

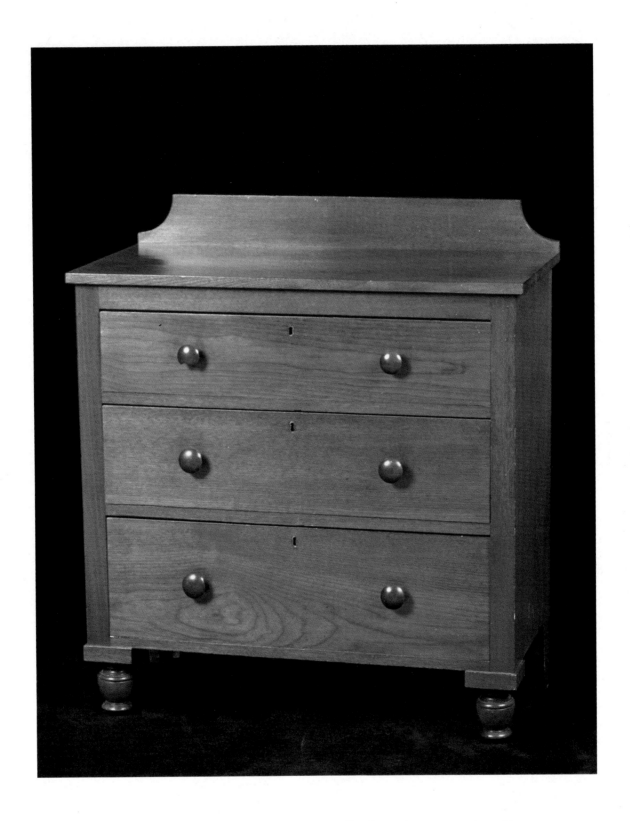

A labeled dresser, probably of the 1870's, that indicates a market with conservative country tastes of some twenty years earlier. The maker was C. S. Seago & Sons, Brantford, Ontario. h. 40", w. 37", d. 19".

(a) The dresser below is Eastlake in form and detail. The base wood of elm is trimmed with cherry. Drawer fronts have ebonized teardrop pulls, wooden escutcheons and bands painted to simulate bird's-eye maple. There is incised carving on the pediment.
This piece matches the bed illustrated on page 36c in *The Marketplace Guide to Oak Furniture*. 1870's - 1880's. h. 86", w. 42", d. 18".

b.

(b) Typically Victorian Renaissance, this dresser is surmounted by an elaborate cresting atop an arched pediment.
The painted surface in almost pristine condition, greatly enhances its value. This painting over a pine base simulates an oak body with walnut veneered panels, decorated with flowers.
The drawers have machine-carved pulls and small lamp brackets flank the mirror.
h. 86", w. 42", d. 19".

a.

a.

b.

c.

(a) A spectacular dresser with an abundance of Victorian Renaissance characteristics. The high crested pediment with carved walnut trim contains a composition-molded female head. Burled walnut is used on portions of the trim, and on raised panels that include a variety of shapes. Solid black walnut is used for the scroll-work, the turned fully-rounded lamp brackets and other moldings. 1860's - 1870's. h. 99", w. 50", d. 18".

(b) A cottage-quality Renaissance dresser with small lamp brackets on the swivel-mirror frame. Originally painted and stenciled. h. 74", w. 38", d. 17".

(c) A dresser in the Eastlake style. The crest has cut-out fretwork. This dresser matches the bed on page 20. h. 84", w. 45", d. 17".

a.

b.

c.

(a) A cottage-quality dresser, this piece would have been painted with stencils and free-hand striping (see 42b). h. 36", w. 39", d. 17".

(b) Another cottage-quality dresser, this one in the Renaissance style, was also ornately painted, stencilled and lined originally (see 42b). h. 84", w. 42", d. 17".

(c) An Eastlake dresser in cottage quality with turned spindles and knops in the cresting. As with the others on this page, it was painted. h. 80", w. 41", d. 18".

A better-quality Eastlake dresser of walnut with fancy-grade walnut
veneer. The cresting has a vaguely Medieval air. The incised
straight lines on the drawer fronts were typical of the type of
carving advocated by Eastlake. The keyhole escutcheons are wood.
1870's - 1880's. h. 86", w. 40", d. 19".

Eastlake in form but with unusual proportions, this exceptionally good piece has a side locking device visible in the brass keyhole escutcheon on the right-hand side. The cresting includes very stylized incised palmettes and flowers. Walnut with walnut veneer. The mirror is beveled.
h. 78", w. 36", d. 20".

The cabinet sections with doors in these dressers could accommodate larger items such as hats or bonnets.

b.

a.

(a) A typical catalog piece of the turn-of-the-century with sparsely-applied carved decorations.
h. 47", w. 32", d. 17".

(b) The assymetrical construction is typical of Eastlake. The chrysanthemum in the door, as well as the fans on the drawers show a strong Japanese influence. h. 61", w. 30", d. 17".

Mail-order houses such as
Sears, Roebuck offered a wide variety of
bedroom suites which usually included a
bed, dresser, and washstand or
"commode". The whole suite was
furnished "complete with casters".

b.

a.

(a) Applied machine carving creates an
ornate cresting on this turn-of-the-century
factory piece. h. 74", w. 44", d. 20".

(b) The dresser above is of late-Victorian
catalog quality. Drawer fronts are
quarter-cut oak veneer and there is
applied carving on the mirror supports.
h. 70", w. 42", d. 23".

Another turn-of-the-century piece, showing the continuing popularity of assymetrical design. The mirror is unusual in that it pivots on two vertical, rather than horizontal points. h. 77", w. 35", d. 17".

For many, the essence of Victorian furniture is a walnut
Rococo arm-chair with a medallion-shaped back and
cabriole legs. These were often made as a part of a
newly-affordable trend — a parlor suite with
gentleman's and lady's chairs, side chairs, a sofa and a
center table. 1850 - 1870.

A Renaissance armchair of walnut with burled-walnut
veneer and incised carving on the frame. The keystone
motif on the crestrail and Pompeiian legs are typical.

CHAIRS   51

a. A late-Victorian Colonial revival with a jumble of styles. From the seat down, it derives from the William and Mary period, but the back relates to later 18th century designs.

b. Another typical walnut Rococo armchair with finger molding on the frame and a balloon back with stylized leaf carvings.

More ornately styled and carved than is common, this Rococo armchair has pronounced scrolled knuckles on the arms and complex shaping to the back frame, including strong C-scrolls at the base.
Late 1840's - 1850's.

a.

b.

(a) A relatively plain Renaissance armchair with rosettes on the back and strongly-turned Pompeiian legs. The apron below the seat rail or skirt is applied, and the squared arm supports enhance the architectural impression.

(b) A popular Victorian revival was the Roman-inspired curule chair. This example includes lions' heads and grotesque masks on its ornately-carved frame.

a. A vaguely Grecian influence can be seen in the scrolled arms and overall feel of this Renaissance chair. Bands of veneer continue all the way down and around the arms.

b. An intricately-carved "lady's chair" in the Renaissance style. Burled-walnut veneer is used in combination with incised carving and attached tassels for decoration. The seat is incurving, and the bun elements on the legs are incised.

a. Bellflowers carved on the back frame are a neoclassical element on this broadly proportioned Renaissance armchair.

b. Possibly made for a dressing table or a hearth corner, the crestrail has simply been lowered on a typical side-chair design.

c. In mahogany, a good colonial revival corner chair of the late 19th century, with pierced back splats and cabriole legs terminating in ball-and-claw feet.

d. Another, more ornate colonial revival corner chair with more exaggerated "knees" on the cabriole legs and heavily knuckled arms.

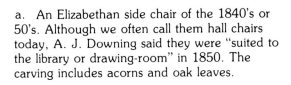

b. Ornate Rococo piercing with C- and S-scrolls dominates this walnut side chair. The cabriole legs also show scrollwork, and the seat is heavily shaped with applied carving in the centre.

a. An Elizabethan side chair of the 1840's or 50's. Although we often call them hall chairs today, A. J. Downing said they were "suited to the library or drawing-room" in 1850. The carving includes acorns and oak leaves.

a.

b.

c.

(a) An Eastlake side chair with Japanese influence, particularly in the stylized chrysanthemum carvings on the back. 1870's -1880's.

(b) Although the overall design is Eastlake, the burled-walnut panels on the skirt and crestrail are a Renaissance influence.

(c) A standard mass-produced Eastlake side chair, with all decorative carving incised.

a. The double cornucopias in the back slat are deeply carved, and the front legs show a modified sabre curve from the klysmos.

b. An elegant Empire chair of mahogany with mahogany-veneer crestrail. The scrolled arms end in a leaf motif. The overall design of the chair shows strong influence of the classical Greek klysmos. 1830's - 1840's.

c.

Detail of slat (b) with carved swans of fine quality.

(c) A narrow-backed colonial-revival sidechair with Queen Anne influence. The back has a lion carved into it, and the seat probably derived from the Windsor family.

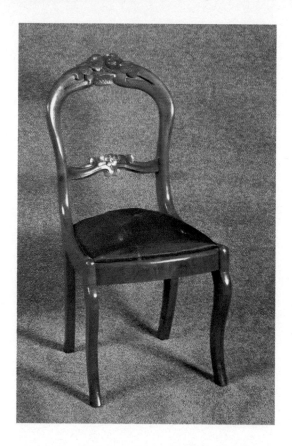

a. An above average mid-Victorian side chair with an attractive carved motif typical of the period.

b. Similar to 60a with sabre legs surviving from the Empire style.

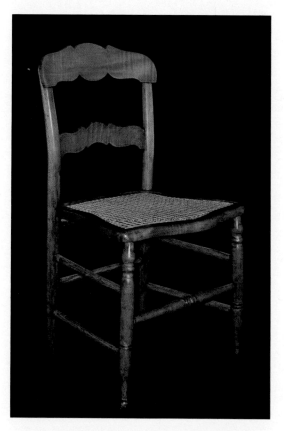

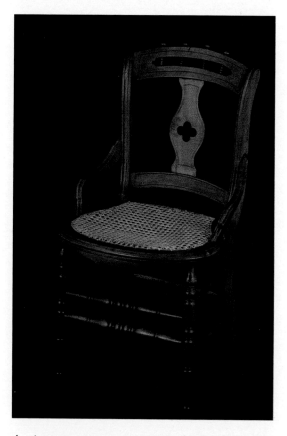

c. A factory-made side chair of typical design with a shaped cane seat. 1870's - 1880's.

d. An inexpensive cane-seated side chair with Renaissance and Eastlake lines, but with a pierced Gothic quatrefoil in the back splat.

a. Cane seated and mass produced, this was intended for desks, offices etc. in the 1870's and 80's.

b. Strong Renaissance influence shows on this version of the desk and office armchair.

c. A walnut side chair of approximately the same vintage and use as the examples above.

d. Although more ornately carved than the example (c), cheaper wood was used.

Crestrails with pressed designs in imitation of carving are called "pressbacks". Few exhibit such intricate details as lions' heads, however. Sears, Roebuck called the round leather seat a "cobbler seat" and such backs are "richly" or "elegantly carved".

a. Labeled "Larkin No. 7", this pressback rocker is typical of late 19th century catalog furniture.

b. Turn of the century. The pierced back was called "fancy shaped" in promotional literature of the time.

c. Late Victorian Oriental influence at its strongest, with a stylized chrysanthemum motif and a dragon in the back.

d. With a full cane seat and back, this was a popular summer-time porch or parlor piece.

a. The solid back splats on this late Victorian rocker were intended to recall the Queen Anne style.

b. The needlepoint is probably original and meant to enhance the "Elizabethan" flavor of this rocker.

c. An inexpensive platform rocker with Eastlake influence in the straight incised line carving, or reeding.

d. The platform mechanism is marked as patented on May 28, 1888 on this Japanese/Eastlake influenced rocker.

The turnings on this rocker retain their original gold paint. The spindles in the back, bamboo-like shaping on the arm supports, and overall angularity are all Japanese/Eastlake characteristics. Upholstery is probably original, and overall it is in excellent shape. 1870's - 1880's.

a. A good early Windsor highchair with original paint and stencilling adding greatly to its value. 1830 - 1850.

b. From the seat up resembling a miniature tavern chair, this Windsor highchair also retains its original paint and stencilling. 1840 - 1860.

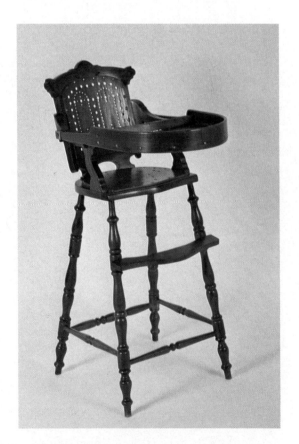

c. Late Victorian with a pierced laminated seat and back and Renaissance shaping to the crestrail. 1870's - 1880's.

d. A typical pressback, the front stretcher shows wear from use after the child's legs could reach it. Turn of the century.

(a) The later 19th century saw many patents for furniture with more than one use. This highchair, manufactured by the A. Merriam Co. of South Acton, Massachusetts, folds to become a rocking chair similar in concept to a rocking horse. The Victorians were a ready market for numerous gimmicks that represented the latest in technology to them.

a.

b.

(b) This illustration shows the chair in the rocking position described above. To achieve this the legs are folded up and out.

a. This piano stool with a back is labeled "A. Merriam Co./South Acton Mass."

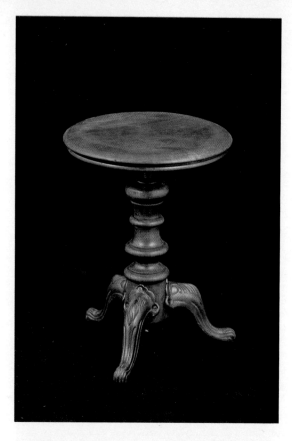

b. These cast-iron legs would have been varnished to resemble the wooden pedestal and seat.

c. Cast-iron legs are attached to a wooden pedestal on this stool, with its original tufted horsehair seat.

d. Busily turned legs support a matching center column on this sturdy example.

(a) Eastlake influence can be seen in the applied apron on this low stool. h. 16", w. 27", d. 27".

(b) Ornately carved, this stool has applied burled-walnut panels and a lift top for storage. h. 20", w. 21", d. 15".

a.

b.

c.

(c) Labeled "The X Piano Tabouret/L. Postawka & Co./Patented April 4, 1871" this stool won medals in the Philadelphia Exposition of 1876 and the Boston Exposition of 1878. The wooden knobs raise and lower the seat level.

(d) A Renaissance stool with an applied roundel on the skirt, and legs with Pompeiian influence.

d.

The terms sofa, couch, lounge, divan, tete-a-tete and settee seem to have meant different things to different writers in the Victorian era. For the sake of simplicity the term sofa is used throughout this section and most writers at that time would probably have agreed that the pieces illustrated fall within that category.

Above is a Rococo sofa with typical curvilinear lines. The carvings on the back and skirt are applied, and the skirt itself is crotch-grained mahogany veneer. The arms are finger molded above strong cabriole legs.

The Empire style is still evident in the straight, crotch-grained mahogany skirt and the flat, scrolled arms and legs. The back, though, with the C- and S-scrolls is strongly Rococo influenced. h. 37", w. 83", d. 24".

a. A late but Empire-influenced piece with flat scrolled arms and legs. The carvings are applied on crotch-grained mahogany veneer.

b. A pure Rococo sofa with typical medallion back. The entire frame is finger-molded walnut with simple stylized fruit-and-leaf carving and cabriole legs. 1850-1860's. h. 38", w. 64".

Another version of the Rococo, this one with a more ornately-carved serpentine back. Walnut, as used on this piece, was the favorite wood in this period. S-scrolled arms are common, as is the serpentine skirt. 1850 - 1860's. h. 38", w. 64".

a. A fine small Eastlake sofa with rectangular lines and complex piercing in the back. The central panel is inlaid with a stylized floral design. h. 41", w. 53", d. 24".

b. Although the overall lines are survival Empire, the detail on this sofa, including the incised carvings and shield motif in the back, are late Renaissance features.

The exaggerated curve to the cabriole legs, the large knuckles on the arms, and the almost "whiplash curves" on the back frame suggest a late 19th century form with Art Nouveau influence.

(a) A fine small davenport desk with a strong Eastlake design. Tiles such as the one centered here in the door were especially popular in the "Arts and Crafts" movement in the later 19th century. Straight incised lines predominate in the carving, and are complemented by the tongue-and-groove construction in the door. Its small size makes it a popular piece today. 1870's -1880's. h. 30", w. 25", d. 20".

a.

(b) The molding on this desks is applied and painted black or "Japanned". The lines are simple but a Renaissance influence can be seen in the applied panel on the drop front.
The pierced gallery almost has an Art Nouveau flavor to the cut-outs.
h. 45", w. 72", d. 19".

b.

A beautiful example of an Eastlake-style cylinder roll-top desk. In walnut with burled-walnut veneer panels, the turnings in the gallery above are repeated in the skirt. The pierced squared cresting above the gallery shows an Oriental influence. Roll-top desks are among the most sought-after pieces of Victorian furniture.

A Renaissance example with burled-walnut panels and a plain gallery.
Probably from the 1870's or 80's, as this type of handle is more likely
to be found on Eastlake pieces.

Simple but elegant lines emphasize the mahogany veneer on this Eastlake cylinder roll-top secretary desk. h. 87", w. 44", d. 24".

a.

(a) Although much the same form as the previous example, this desk shows more of a Renaissance influence in the applied carvings and moldings. The case is walnut with burled-walnut veneer.

(b) A drop-front secretary desk with Renaissance detail in the applied veneered panels and roundels.

b.

Desks possibly vary in design more than any other form, from small "ladies" desks to the massive and rare "Wooten's Patent Desk" of the 1870's and 80's. The latter was the predecessor of today's self-contained modular furniture with a variety of compartments including its own letter box.

b.

a.

(a) A straightforward Eastlake design of the 1870's with multiple incised lines of reeding as the predominant decoration. h. 48", w. 29".

(b) Probably cabinetmaker made, this cherry desk shows a survival-Empire influence in the S-scrolled supports, but the original fruit-and-leaf handles were factory made and are of the Renaissance period, thus dating the piece that late.

A massive desk of imposing proportions. Design elements are mainly Victorian Elizabethan, with heavy "barleytwist" stiles and intricately-paneled doors. The handles, however, are copies of those found on more ornate Chippendale pieces. h. 30", w. 63", d. 36".

(a) An unusually-designed Renaissance desk, possibly a special order. A variety of fancy-grained woods are used, including crotch-grained mahogany, bird's-eye and tiger maple, and burled walnut. h. 34", w. 47", d. 22".

The spacious interior is shown, with well-executed scalloping on the four pigeon holes.

(a) Made for an office, this "partners" desk is very plain with machine-carved fruit-and-leaf handles relieving the stark lines. h. 33", w. 52", d. 39".

a.

b. A pine country version of the "roll-top" form. This desk was made without the actual rolling curtain. h. 49", w. 40", d. 22".

c. Standard office furniture of the late 19th century, this factory-made walnut example is still very popular today. h. 47", w. 48", d. 29".

An attractive Renaissance bookcase in walnut with applied burled-walnut panels. As with previous pieces, its small proportions make it a desirable piece in today's rooms. h. 58", w. 38", d. 9".

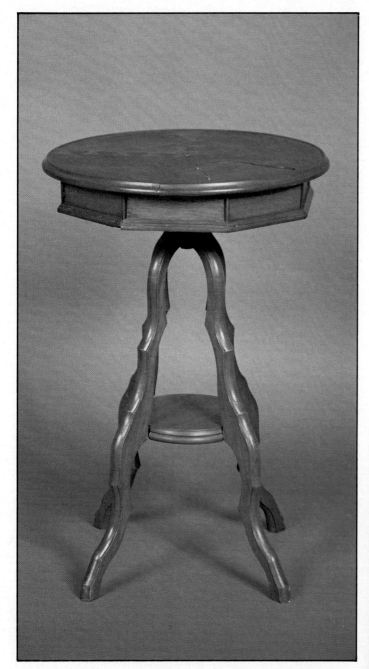

a.

Sewing tables were usually called "work tables" in the 19th century, as a woman might use them for a variety of handwork projects besides sewing. These tables were usually small and easily moved to be in the best light.

b.

(a) A sewing table with complexly-fitted panels dovetailing together to form the revolving top. A hinged piece in the top opens into the compartment below as it revolves. The legs show a Renaissance influence and it is marked as patented July 18, 1871.

(b) Mahogany and mahogany veneer accentuate this fine sewing table. The silk bag below pulls out like a drawer to hold knitting and other work. h. 30", w. 27", d. 19".

a.

b.

c.

(a) Survival Sheraton is evident in this simple, attractive table with tiger maple used in the top, front and legs. h. 26", w. 19", d. 17".

(b) A fine Empire sewing or work table with ogee-shaped top drawer, mahogany veneered carcass and tiger-maple top. 1835 - 1850. h. 28", w. 22", d. 17".

(c) A small spool-turned walnut table of cottage quality with a shaped top showing Renaissance influence. h. 25", w. 23", d. 13".

a. An Eastlake plant or lamp stand with a marble top. The finish is original, and retains some gold detailing. h. 32", w. 17", d. 17".

b. A cottage-quality Renaissance piece, this was originally painted and stencilled.
h. 30", w. 24", d. 16".

c. Rococo vine-and-leaf designs form the cast-iron legs on this walnut occasional table.

d. A typical small drop-leaf pedestal table in the Renaissance style. 1860's - 1870's.

(a) This Renaissance pedestal table in walnut features incised carving on the four legs and a turned drop on the central supporting column. 1860-1880.

a.

(b) A variation of (a), the angular incised carving on the sides of the legs and the apron, together with the reeding on the leg's edge, are Eastlake details. h. 30", w. 29", d. 20".

b.

a. With burled-walnut veneer, this table is above average for turn-of-the-century furniture. h. 29", w. 38", d. 25".

b.

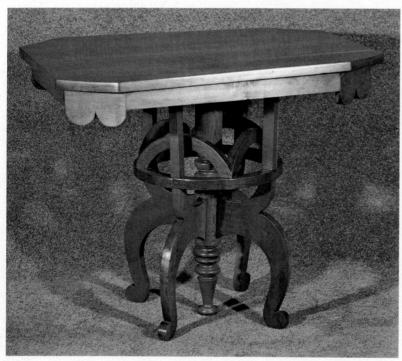

c.

(b) Brass beads and urn shapes are meant as Colonial details on this table which appears in the 1901 Eaton's catalog.

(c) A decidedly individual piece in cherry. The shaping of the top and skirt are the only typical late-Victorian features on it. h. 27", w. 33", d. 24".

a. Eastlake parlor tables in the "Japanese taste" often had small shelves below the top to display bric-a-brac including Oriental objects. h. 29", w. 32", d. 20".

b. A very attractive Eastlake piece, with well-designed fretwork in the stretchers. This may have served as a parlor or breakfast table.

c. This parlor table shows another interpretation of the Eastlake style. The top is brown marble and the aprons on the skirt have a fan-like design.

d. A later 19th century colonial revival or centennial piece. The swags on the skirt and slim-turned legs with columnar tops are meant as neoclassical details.

a.

Practicality has made tilt-top tables popular for centuries. The top is often of finer wood making a polished showing even in their tilted position. They may range in size from small candle stands to breakfast tables.

(a) A single piece of mahogany forms the top of this excellent quality tilt-top pedestal table.
h. 29", w. 30", d. 36".

(b) Another tilt-top with a butternut top, this country piece has four rather than the usual three legs supporting the central pedestal.
h. 29", dia. 43".

b.

Extension tables were popular throughout the Victorian era. At first they were most often found as finer pieces suitable for affluent dining rooms but by the end of the century, they were popular items in the mail-order catalogs.

a. An Eastlake pedestal-base dining table in walnut with Japanese-derived fans on the upper legs and incised carving. w. 47", d. 48".

b. Another Eastlake dining table, but with more "medieval" styling to it. The heavy turned legs and incised central roundel were felt to reflect "ancient" designs.

a. A simple country survival-Sheraton kitchen table of a type
which continued throughout the Victorian era. This example has a
two-board top on which the corners have been trimmed at some
point in time. h. 30", w. 58", d. 33".

b. Survival-Empire styling shows in the heavy octagonal turned legs of
this late Victorian dining table. A popular style over many years, the
oval top can extend for several feet with the extension of leaves.
w. 60", d. 45".

Like tilt-top and extension tables, drop-leaf tables were an answer to the problem of space. Many rooms might have more than one use and in smaller households, the parlor could serve as a dining room on more-formal occasions.

(a) A pine topped drop-leaf of the later 19th century with heavy turned legs. The legs have been shortened and it was probably originally stained to resemble a better wood.
h. 28", w. 45", d. 49".

(b) Bird's-eye maple makes up all the visible wood on this piece. The leaf is made from two boards, and the legs have been cut down, probably when the casters were added.

(c) This drop-leaf has a cherry top and Sheraton legs that are slightly finer than the previous examples, possibly indicating an earlier date.
h. 29", w. 48", d. 51".

Domestic encyclopedias of the 19th century suggested that servers, or serving tables, were useful in the dining room to augment the sideboard as a place to put dirty dishes. It was suggested that the server be placed against a wall opposite the sideboard for balance. In smaller homes, they might replace the sideboard.

a. A hall or serving table in Renaissance style with incised carving showing Eastlake influence.

b. A fine example of imitation mahogany graining. The original finish greatly enhances the value here. Mid-1830's - 1850. h. 37", w. 34", d. 17".

c. A late-19th century serving table in revival "Colonial" Empire style. h. 47", w. 44", d. 20".

(a) The craftsman who built this sideboard had a good understanding of the concepts of furniture design promoted by Charles Locke Eastlake. The overall effect is restrained, and the delicate incised carving is the type of detail Eastlake shows in *Hints on Household Taste*.
h. 48", w. 54", d. 21".

a.

(b) A variety of woods including maple and ash went into this individually-produced sideboard. The scrollwork supports show a survival-Empire influence and the overall effect of the piece is one of massiveness.
h. 48", w. 63", d. 26".

b.

An Eastlake sideboard with complexly-shaped elaborate cresting. h. 84", w. 48", d. 21".

High-backed sideboards are more likely to be found in the later Victorian styles. Their massive proportions were well suited to the high ceilings in most houses of the period, and they lent an imposing air to formal dinners. h. 84", w. 48", d. 21".

A good Renaissance example with strong architectural elements and rather unusual decorative details in the pediment and on the panels. Probably made as a special order. Cherry and walnut with burled-walnut veneer. 1870's - 1880's. h. 94", w. 60", d. 19".

a. The Renaissance details, including applied handles and surrounding cartouche, enliven this otherwise simple, country piece. h. 94", w. 46", d. 22".

b. A relatively simple Renaissance sideboard with a marble top. The arched pediment has an applied cartouche with a central cabochon which is repeated on the doors. h. 76", w. 38", d. 21".

a.

Mail-order catalogs usually offered a variety of sideboards like this. Although they might vary in applied details or carved outlines, the general form was often identical.

(a) A late 19th century factory piece with heavy applied machine carvings in oak. Casters were standard on many mail-order pieces. h. 76", w. 46", d. 20".

(b) Mainly oak veneer with applied carvings. This turn-of-the-century sideboard has a stylized pineapple on its cresting and, as the catalogs termed it, a "serpentine shaped top". h. 78", w. 45", d. 21".

b.

a.

b.

c.

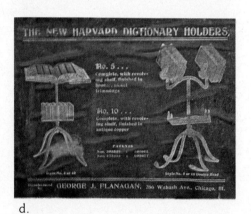

d.

Small miscellaneous items lend a period air to rooms with Victorian decor.

(a) & (d) A dictionary stand with label illustrated.

(b) Music stand with cast-iron base with Oriental influence.

(c) A good Eastlake magazine rack with scalloped skirt. h. 33", w. 19".

(e) Shoeshine box with a hint of Eastlake incised beading.

(f) A folding gout stool. Gout was considered a disease of the affluent in Victoria's day, and stools such as this were fashionable.

e.

f.

a. A small but heavily-decorated mirror with Renaissance lines. The raised carving is applied. Both the raised and incised carving relate to machine-produced drawer pulls of fruit-and-leaf designs.

b. Eastlake motifs are incised into this late 19th century medicine cabinet with attached towel racks. The 1897 Sears, Roebuck catalog says that similar pieces are "for bathroom or office", and stresses the "beautiful French bevel plate mirror" as a selling point.

c. The composition-molded bust of a nobleman of the Italian Renaissance emphasizes the Renaissance styling of this small shelf. As in 103a, the carving is both applied and incised, a combination common on pieces of this period.

(d) A very high quality renaissance shaving stand. A gentleman could keep his razors and towels in the drawer and the shaving mug and brush on the marble shelf. Of course, he would stand to shave using the small tilting mirror.
h. 62", w. 17", d. 16".

(e) Another small shaving stand with a drawer only large enough to hold razors. This piece has emphatic Elizabethan revival turnings. Shaving stands of the same general form as these two are also occasionally found in cast iron as well.
h. 62", w. 15", d. 15".

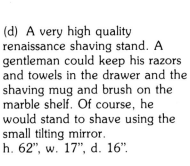

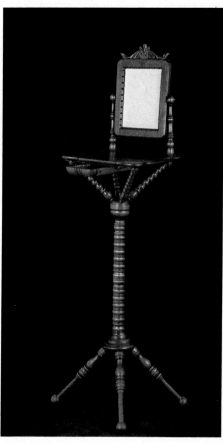

d.

e.

A fine hallstand with a brass hatrack above as well as hooks.
The elaborate carvings include faces on the arm supports and in
the centre back. Late 19th century. h. 80", w. 36", d. 16".

a. An excellent Renaissance dressing mirror with an arched pediment above a small dentil molding. This piece could be used today in a vestibule or entrance hall. In a larger area, it might serve to reflect a luxuriant plant on a Victorian fern stand. h. 88", w. 52".

c. A good quality late Renaissance pier mirror. The three small platforms above may have held anything from stuffed birds to Oriental vases.

b. This later 19th century hall mirror has stylized-griffin cutouts on the base. h. 81", w. 24", d. 9".

a. A Renaissance hallstand in cast iron with ornate Rococo floral detail. A fine example of North American casting of the 1850's or 60's.

b. A late-19th century hallstand with seat enclosing storage below it. The incised carvings show a vaguely Oriental influence.

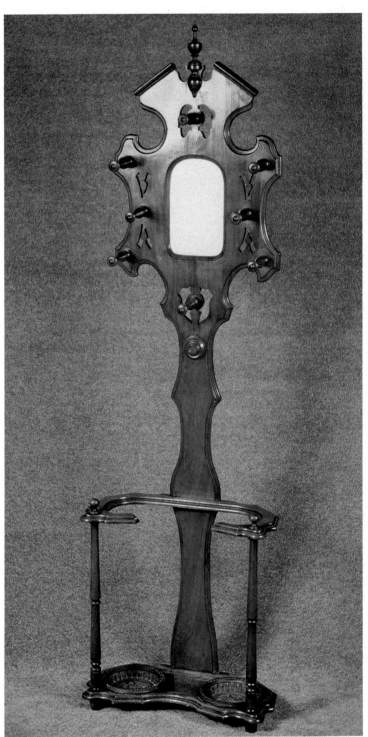

b. A Renaissance hallstand surmounted by a
broken pediment with central turned finial.
1860-1880. h. 84", w. 25", d. 12".

a. A cottage-quality Renaissance hallstand
with cutout fretwork on the mirror surround.
h. 80", w. 28", d. 11".

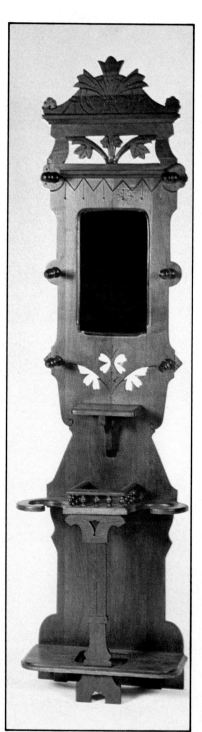

a. This fine Eastlake hallstand includes marble drawer-top and complex machine-cut detail. h. 80", w. 31", d. 10".

b. A simpler Eastlake hallstand with fretwork flowers showing Japanese influence. h. 84", w. 24", d. 9".

c. An assymetrical "Japanese Eastlake" hallstand with thin decorative spindles. h. 78", w. 30", d. 11".

a. An unusual what-not or étagère of spindle and ball turnings.

b. Another with spindle and ball turnings, but further enhanced by a bentwood lyre. 1880's or 90's.

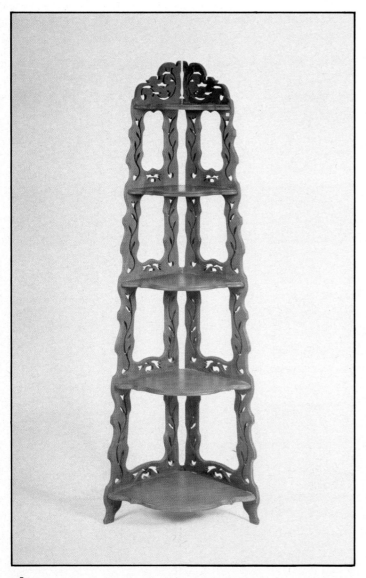

a.

c.

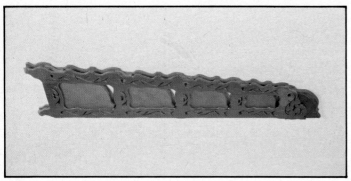

b.

(a) This "Folding Book Stand" in the Renaissance style was patented in 1872 by David Heald of Milford, N.H. h. 66", w. 20".

(b) 110a is shown folded for storage or shipping.

(c) A very attractive Renaissance what-not with well-designed piercing. h. 61", w. 23".

a. A simple corner what-not with well-turned supports. h. 54", w. 26".

b. This example has typical Renaissance shaping to the cutouts. h. 61", w. 23".

c. A virtuoso fretwork piece with bracket feet and applied carving on the shelf aprons. h. 72", w. 36".

d. Notable features of this example are the spool or sausage turnings and pierced gallery. h. 57", w. 29".

◁ A beautiful, fine-quality étagère with marble
table top. The overall shaping and leg
design is Rococo, but the fretwork cut-outs
on the sides are a Renaissance detail. The
carving on the apron is applied.

The Victorian Era

The Victorian Era, like any age of mankind, was one of contradictions. They were visible everywhere from the structure of society itself to the design and structure of its furniture. The romantic and the pragmatic, nostalgia for the past and fascination with technological and social progress were intermingled without a trace of self-consciousness. Sir Walter Scott's novel of by-gone days and dashing knighthood, *Ivanhoe*, stood side-by-side on many Victorian bookshelves with Charles Dickens' indictment of social evils and plea for reform, *Oliver Twist*. This dichotomy is particularly evident in the industrial and trade exhibitions which were the rage of the entire era, and spread from the Continent to England to America. Two of the most famous, The Crystal Palace Exhibition of 1851 in England and the Centennial Exhibition of 1876 in the United States, stand out especially.

The marriage of the young Queen Victoria to Prince Albert had captured the imagination of the English-speaking world. "Yankees" eagerly questioned English visitors to their shores about the couple. Their honeymoon, every detail of their public lives, and as much as could be ascertained of their private lives was printed and re-printed by the press.

EXTERIOR OF THE BUILDING FOR THE GREAT EXHIBITION (SOUTH SIDE).

The Queen was lovely; the Prince handsome. Their marriage was played upon for readers who were eager for the romance of young royalty. But beneath the penny-newspaper facade were two people who proved to be intelligent, capable, and perceptive.

Albert, from the first, was deeply interested in trade and technology. He saw clearly that Great Britain's future depended on commerce and industrial development, and that Britain's advances must be made visible to the world. France had hosted a number of successful industrial expositions, and the Prince proposed, in 1848, that Great Britain sponsor an exhibition of industry from all nations of the world. Over the next few years he encountered antipathy and opposition, but his perseverance finally created a climate of popular enthusiasm for the idea that led to its approval. On May 1st, 1851, Queen Victoria opened *The Great Exhibition of the Industry of All Nations.* The building that housed the Exhibition was in itself a monument of technology. Designed by Joseph Paxton, it seemed a fantastic "crystal palace" to many who entered it, and the name was soon

attached to it. The huge glass-and-iron structure glistened in the sunlight. The main section was 1848 feet long and 408 feet wide, and when the visitor entered he found himself in the dazzling 108 foot-high transept. Yet the Crystal Palace's design was, in fact, highly practical for the type of exhibition it housed. Difficulties in construction and erection had been carefully thought out and minimized. The exhibits called for a tremendous amount of light to be shown off to their fullest, and only an incredibly large square footage of glass would allow such illumination. Within, heavy machinery vied with the latest furniture designs and boomerangs from Australia for attention. It was the quintessential mixture of the strange, the romantic, the practical, and the innovative.

Exhibitions did not cease with the Crystal Palace. In fact, it seemed to give them a new impetus. Paris saw several more, and the United States followed suit with one in New York in 1853, and those in Louisville and Cincinnati in 1872. These were, to an extent, "trial balloons" for the big one in the works: the 1876 Centennial in Philadelphia.

The years prior to 1876 had not been easy for the United States. The Civil War had been over for only eleven years, and it had left deep scars. At the time of the Centennial, re-construction was still in effect and bitter feelings remained between the North and South. A few years earlier, the country had suffered a brief but unnerving depression, and the scandals of financial mismanagement during Ulysses S. Grant's presidency were continuing to make headlines.

In the midst of this, the American people longed for an affirmation of their traditional values and heritage (there was a tremendous interest in George Washington's personal possessions displayed at the Exhibition). At the same time, they needed re-assurance about their future in a fast-changing world. The Centennial Exhibition helped answer both of these needs. Perhaps reflecting their consciousness of Westward expansion across the continent, size seemed to be of paramount importance. One "Historical Register of the Centennial Exposition" details the comparative acreage of land covered by all previous exhibitions and the present one. Needless to say, it far outstripped its precedessors. The main building, of glass and iron, like London's, had basic dimensions of 1880 feet by 464 feet

— just overshadowing the former's size. It was not, however, limited to this single building. Four other large structures — The Art Gallery, Machinery Hall, Horticultural Hall, and The Agricultural Building, were also joined by almost 200 other buildings, including many pavilions of foreign countries. They housed everything you could imagine, from "Campbell's New Rotary Perfecting - Press" to exotic dancers in the "Tunisian Cafe". A supposed re-creation of an early log cabin, with a sign over the door reading "Ye Olden Time/Welcome to All", was packed with a muddle of colonial and not-so-colonial furnishings. This exhibit helped to spark the enthusiasm for "Colonial Revival" furniture that has continued into this century. Other exhibits made an impact as well. Japan had a huge pavilion, and the display of Japanese decorative arts encouraged the fascination with Oriental motifs which appear, especially in Eastlake furniture, for years after. In fact, many of the pieces in this book reflect romantic revival or "exotic" styles that were made popular through the displays of furniture manufacturers at Expositions. But even if the design recalls an earlier era or a faraway land, the construction methods may, at the same time, be the offspring of the other face of the Victorian Age — industry and progress.

Styles and Influences

Although the phrase "Victorian Furniture" brings to mind for many the sinuous curves of the Rococo and the monumental size of the Renaissance Revival, Victoria's reign encompassed a much greater variety of styles, from late Sheraton and Empire in the early years to Mission by the turn of the 20th century. It took time for new styles to be assimilated, and often details from an older style would be combined with the latest fashion, creating a "transitional" piece. Also, many styles were popular concurrently, so that it is impossible to devise a strictly chronological order. Sometimes a particular *form* continued to be popular in a style that was otherwise outdated. For example, kitchen work tables with light, simply-turned legs influenced by the Sheraton style of the early 19th century were made well into the 20th. These forms are termed "survival" pieces, and are typically found in country furniture. Other styles had a lesser influence, and are to be seen only in ornamental details, or as specific forms. Such is the case, for instance, with the Gothic style, most often found fully developed in side chairs and as decorative components elsewhere.

From the above, it is obvious that the dating spans given here can only be approximate. Many styles are known today by more than one name. Some of these are modern terms, and some are Victorian. Where several names are common, the alternates are mentioned after the one used in the text.

Major Styles

Sheraton — 1800-1840's

Generally much earlier than Victorian, this style, named after cabinetmaker and designer Thomas Sheraton, appears in "Survival" pieces, particularly in country furniture. Relatively thin, turned round legs with or without ornamentation are the most common feature associated with Sheraton today.

Empire — 1830's - '50's
(Pillar and Scroll, American Empire, Restoration)

Originally derived from French designs featuring classical Greek, Roman and Egyptian motifs, the Empire style in North America owes a great deal more to the newly-felt influence of machinery in the workshop. A feeling of mass and weight with plain, flat C- and S-scrolled elements characterize it. Surfaces are often undecorated except for the grain of the wood, and crotch-grained mahogany veneered on pine predominates. The classical Greek *klysmos* form of chair, with its outcurved "sabre" legs, is still seen, but rarely as an exact stylistic copy.

Gothic — 1830's - '60's

Although Gothic revival architecture developed immense popularity at this time, furniture in the style gained less of a foothold. Most commonly found are hall stands and side chairs with pointed arched backs, steeple-shaped finials and pierced fretwork or "tracery" with quatrefoil and trefoil motifs. The style is also visible in the pointed arched panels in glazed doors on bookcases, desks, etc. Other forms, such as armchairs and benches, were made for specific buildings in the Gothic style. Lesser pieces were sometimes combined with spool turning (see below).

Spool Turned and Cottage — 1830's - '80's
(Bobbin or Sausage-turned, Elizabethan)

The complex spiral twistings of Elizabethan and early 17th century furniture served as a vague inspiration for the simplified, machine-produced spool turnings that swept North America. Today, the "Jenny Lind" bed is the most immediately recognized form of spool turning.

Cottage furniture denoted not only this particular style, but a quality as well. Inexpensive pieces, made of lesser woods painted and decorated, continued to be called "Cottage" well into the century. Cottage bedroom suites in the Renaissance Revival were especially popular.

Rococo — late 1840's - '60's
(Louis XV, French Antique)

The most recognized of the romantic revivals. The complex curves of the Rococo recall the furniture of the reign of Louis XV in the mid-18th century. A complete departure from the plain, flat surfaces of the Empire style, the Rococo features ornate raised carving (often machine produced) with swags of grapes, pears, foliage, etc. Deeply scooped finger molding usually outlines upholstery, broken at points by stylized fruit, leaves and flowers. Visible wood is one continuous flow of C- and S- or cyma-curves and scrolls. S-curved cabriole legs appear on tables, chairs, sofas and footstools. Parlor suites, sometimes with a large variety of pieces, were popular.

Renaissance — 1850 -'70's
(Louis XVI)

Designs adapted from Renaissance architecture give this style a rectilinear feel. Headboards of beds, backs on sideboards and washstands, all with variations on the pediment, remind one of ornate Renaissance doorways. Carved decoration is often raised, and includes swags of fruit and long cartouches of applied molding. Panels of burled-walnut are veneered on many pieces, although they are sometimes found to be only grained paint. Vase- and steeple-shaped finials (pointing up) and drops (pointing down) are common. Chairs and tables have Pompeiian legs, with a large bun-turned element above a slender, turned tapered column. Round applied bosses and roundels are typical motifs, with simple incised lines. Pieces in walnut are often decorated with ebonizing and touched with gold paint. Cottage-quality pieces are completely painted, sometimes in imitation of better woods (see Spool Turned and Cottage).
The Renaissance style was later mixed with Eastlake (see below).

Eastlake — 1870 - '90's
(Jacobean, Japanese)

Named after Charles Locke Eastlake, author of *Hints on Household Taste,* first published in 1868. Eastlake was a reformer in design, and allied philosophically with a movement advocating a return to the relative simplicity of medieval designs. Sometimes called the Arts and Crafts movement, it included William Morris and John Ruskin amongst its supporters. Eastlake disliked the complex and massive carvings of the Rococo and Renaissance revivals, and illustrated plainer, more angular pieces. Carving is incised or cut in, rather than raised in high relief. Simple, straight lines of beading are used on drawer fronts, legs and backboards. When floral motifs do appear, they are sparse, stylized incised vines with small flowers and leaves. Roundels and bosses are used sparingly, and many pieces have galleries and skirts of small turned spindles. Eastlake pieces sometimes show Japanese influence, with assymetrically placed fans, chrysanthemums, etc. Ebonizing is found on some pieces, and Medieval or Japanese decorated ceramic tiles are set into washstands and sideboards. Tables sometimes have "gingerbread" cut aprons, and backboards on other pieces are similarly cut. As the Renaissance style overlapped the Eastlake chronologically, details from both are often mingled in one piece.

Oak — 1880's - 1900's

Late in the century the mail-order houses such as Sears, Roebuck had a massive impact on the furniture industry. Mass production had reached a new height, and oak was the wood most favored. The necessity for shipping furniture long distances called for some practical modifications in design, and although one can find a real pot-pourri of decorative elements from earlier revivals, overall form is usually fairly simple. Many woods other than oak were used in this period, but they were commonly painted and grained or, later, printed to resemble oak. The desire for a *feeling* of massiveness continues, even if the boards themselves were thinner than in earlier years.

Mission — late 1890's - 1900's
(Craftsman)

In the late 1890's Mission furniture appeared on the market and met with an enthusiastic response. Two major designers, Gustav Stickley (who called it "Craftsman" furniture) and Elbert Hubbard, led the field. However, there was a great emphasis on home production, and many "how-to" books were published on Mission furniture. Simple to the extreme, it was an ideal project for the handyman. Although other woods were used, oak was the most popular. Heavy, square-cut supporting elements enclose flat slats giving a squared, intentionally "primitive" look that at times feels quite modern. Leather or oil-cloth cushions were typically used.

Other Trends and Influences

Country — entire period
(Survival, Primitive, Vernacular)

While formal styles dominated the factories and most cabinetmakers' shops, there were many pieces made by carpenters, skilled laymen, and even cabinetmakers in smaller towns which show much less of this influence. Simple, practical furniture may well owe more to the individual craftsman for its design than to the popular mode. As well, some formal styles remained in vogue much longer in more conservative communities, creating "survival" pieces.

Cast Iron — 1840's - 1890's

By the 1840's, entire storefronts were being produced of cast iron, ready to be shipped and assembled. Furniture in the Gothic and Rococo styles, made for both indoors and out, was popular by mid-century. Hall stands, umbrella stands, fire screens, mirror frames, plant stands and beds were all produced, but beds remained fashionable longest, culminating in the iron and brass extravaganzas of the turn of the century.

Bentwood — 1860's - 1900's

Michael Thonet (rhymes with bonnet) and his factory in Vienna, Austria can be credited with perfecting large-scale production of bentwood furniture. Many of the forms still popular today had been developed by the mid-1860's, including the standard restaurant chair and the rocker.

Colonial Revival — 1870's - 1900's
(Centennial)

Post-Civil War nostalgia for earlier, more stable days, coupled with the 1876 U.S. Centennial celebrations led to an interest in antiques and "Colonial" styles. Varying from carefully-copied accuracy to a mish-mash of elements of several periods in one piece, most examples lean towards the latter. Finer pieces however, with decades of wear on them, may be confused with originals.

L'Art Nouveau — 1880's - 1900's

Although little furniture was made in North America which was totally in this style, the elongated "whiplash" curves and female forms with flowing hair and clothing did influence decorative detail as the century drew to a close.

Windsor Chairs — entire period

Any chair with a spindle back and legs that socket into a solid plank seat can lay claim to being a member of the Windsor family. Beginning in England in the early 18th century, they quickly developed in North America as well. Victorian Windsors often show stylistic influences from more formal furniture, as in the Empire feel of the scrollwork on the Boston rocker.

Who's Who

You may find, in your travels, a few names mentioned by dealers and collectors that are not among those already discussed in the "Styles and Influences" section. Some of these designers, manufacturers, etc. of the period are listed below.

Belter, John Henry: The foremost manufacturer of Rococo furniture in America. He patented a method of laminating wood (usually rosewood) which was then finished with ornate pierced carving.

Downing, Andrew Jackson: published *The Architecture of Country Houses* in 1850. The section on furniture greatly influenced taste at the time.

Godey, L.A.: produced a popular periodical, *Godey's Lady's Book,* which contained sections on homes and furnishings.

Hall, John: a Baltimore architect who published *The Cabinetmaker's Assistant* in 1840. This was a major contribution to the popularity of the Empire style in America.

Jacques and Hay: a large furniture manufacturing firm based in Toronto, Ontario. Pieces in the Renaissance and Eastlake styles are often indiscriminately attributed to them, and those styles are even called "Jacques and Hay" on occasion.

Larkin, John: founder of a huge commercial empire which included furniture manufacturing in the late 19th century. A major catalogue sales establishment.

Loudon, J.C.: published *The Encyclopaedia of Cottage, Farm and Villa Architecture and Furniture* in 1833. Another trend-setter in furniture design.

Meeks, Joseph: a New York cabinetmaker who pioneered the Empire style in America with a major illustrated advertisement in 1833.

Bibliography

Reprints

The number of reprints of 19th century design books, furniture catalogues, etc. is increasing daily. Many of these are really enjoyable reading, and provide an excellent first-hand look at the period.

Asher and Adams. *Pictorial Album of American Industry - 1876.* New York: Rutledge Books, 1976

Baird, Henry Carey. *Victorian Gothic and Renaissance Revival Furniture.* Philadelphia: The Athenaeum of Philadelphia, 1977

Blackie and Son. *The Victorian Cabinet-maker's Assistant* (1853). New York: Dover Publications, 1970

Catalogue of *The Great Exhibition of London 1851* (Crystal Palace). New York: Crown Publishers, Inc., 1970 and New York: Dover Publications, 1970

Downing, A.J. *The Architecture of Country Houses.* New York: Dover Publications, 1969

Eastlake, Charles L. *Hints on Household Taste* (1872 edition). New York: Dover Publications, 1969

Klimsch, Karl. *Florid Victorian Ornament.* New York: Dover Publications, 1977 (not a furniture book, but containing common Victorian design motifs).

Loudon, J.C. and Downing, A.J. *Furniture for the Victorian Home.* Watkins Glen, New York: American Life Foundation Study Institute, 1978 (reprints of Loudon's *Encyclopaedia* of 1833 and Downing's *Country Houses* of 1850).

Montgomery Ward and Co. *Catalogues for 1894 and 1895.* Northfield, Illinois: Gun Digest, 1970 and *1895 Catalog* New York: Dover Publications, 1969

Sears, Roebuck, *Catalog (1897).* New York: Chelsea House Publishers, 1968

Sears, Roebuck *Catalog (Fall 1900).* Northfield, Illinois, Digest Books, 1970

Sheraton, Thomas. *The Cabinet-Maker and Upholsterer's Drawing Book.* New York: Dover Publications, 1972

Stickley, Gustav. *Craftsman Furniture Catalogs.* New York: Dover Publications, 1979

The T. Eaton Co. *Catalogue (1901).* Toronto: The Musson Book Co., 1970

Wooten Desk Company. *Catalog (1876).* New York: Wooten Desk Collection, Inc. (no pub. date).

Glossaries

A few definitions are given in the glossary at the front. The books below are full-scale reference works.

Aronson, Joseph. *The Encyclopedia of Furniture.* New York: Crown Publishers, Inc. 1938

Boger, Louise Ade and Batterson. *The Dictionary of Antiques and the Decorative Arts.* New York: Charles Scribner's Sons, 1957

Fleming, John and Honour, Hugh. *The Penguin Dictionary of Decorative Arts.* New York: Penguin Books, 1979

Pegler, Martin. *The Dictionary of Interior Design.* New York: Crown Publishers, 1966

Period Interiors

These include sketches, photographs, etc. of 19th century rooms done at the time. Useful not only to date pieces, but to get a feel for the era.

Byron, Joseph. *Photographs of New York Interiors at the Turn of the Century.* New York: Dover Publications, 1976

Peterson, Harold. *American Interiors from Colonial Times to the Late Victorians.* New York: Charles Scribner's Sons, 1971

Seale, William. *The Tasteful Interlude: American Interiors Through the Camera's Eye, 1860-1917.* New York: Praeger Publishers, 1975

Construction Methods

The knowledge of the different methods of construction which were used at different periods, and by individual cabinetmakers versus factories, can help immensely in dating pieces, spotting fakes, and evaluating quality.

Koltun, L.A. *The Cabinetmaker's Art in Ontario c. 1850-1900.* Ottawa, Ontario. National Museums of Canada, 1979. (Contains an excellent discussion of the furniture industry, and recognizing cabinetmaker's work vs. factory work.)

Smith, Nancy A. *Old Furniture: Understanding the Craftsman's Art.* Boston and Toronto. Little, Brown & Co., 1975 (Although dealing mainly with early pieces, it does contain discussion of later methods.)

Voss, Thomas M. *The Bargain Hunter's Guide to Used Furniture.* New York: Dell Publishing Co., 1980

(see also Periodicals: *Fine Woodworking* and *The Chronicle*).

General

Agius, Pauline. *British Furniture 1880-1915.* Woodbridge, Suffolk, England: Antique Collector's Club, 1978

Andrews, John. *The Price Guide to Victorian Furniture.* Woodbridge, Suffolk, England: Antique Collector's Club, 1973

Bishop, Robert. *Guide to American Antique Furniture.* New York: Galahad Books, 1973

Blundell, Peter. *The Marketplace Guide to Oak Furniture.* Paducah, Kentucky: Collector Books, 1980

Bridgeman, Harriet and Drury, Elizabeth. *The Encyclopedia of Victoriana,* New York: Macmillan, 1975

Butler, Joseph T. *American Furniture.* London, Triune Books, 1973

Denker, Ellen and Bert. *The Rocking Chair Book.* New York: Mayflower Books, 1979

Fales, Dean A. Jr. *American Painted Furniture 1660-1880.* New York: E. P. Dutton and Co. Inc., 1979

Gaines, Edith and Jenkins, Dorothy H. *The Woman's Day Dictionary of Antique Furniture.* New York: Hawthorn Books, 1974

Honour, Hugh. *Cabinet Makers and Furniture Designers.* New York: Hamlyn Publishing Group, Ltd., 1972

Joy, Edward T. *English Furniture 1800-1851.* Toronto: Fitzhenry & Whiteside, 1977

Madigan, Mary Jean Smith. *Eastlake-Influenced American Furniture 1870-1890.* Yonkers, New York: The Hudson River Museum, 1974

Ormsbee, Thomas H. *Field Guide to American Victorian Furniture.* New York: Bonanza Books, 1952

Otto, Celia Jackson. *American Furniture of the Nineteenth Century.* New York: The Viking Press, 1965

Periodicals

Canadian Collector. 27 Carlton St., Suite 406, Toronto, Ontario, M5B 1L2 (A general antiques magazine with regular articles on furniture.)

The Chronicle. Early American Industries Association, c/o John S. Kebabian, 2 Winding Lane, Scarsdale, N.Y. 10583. (Excellent articles on construction methods and early cabinetmaking.)

Fine Woodworking. The Tauton Press, P.O. Box 355, Newtown, Connecticut 06470 (Aimed mainly at advanced woodworkers, contains numerous articles on early construction methods, styles, etc.)

The Magazine Antiques. 551 Fifth Avenue, New York, N.Y. 10017. (Often contains articles on styles, makers, important collections, etc.)

Nineteenth Century. c/o Salmagundi Club, 47 Fifth Avenue, New York, N.Y. 10003. (The magazine of the Victorian Society of America).

Index

Co-Author

Peter Blundell is the author of
The Marketplace Guide to Oak Furniture.
He was born and educated in England and
after studying retail distribution at London City
and Guilds, he was employed on Savile Row.
He has travelled extensively in Europe, and
overland across the American Continent. He
lived on the West Coast and in Quebec before
settling in Ontario.

Peter, with his wife Marian operate an antique
shop in the village of Schomberg. He has
worked at flea markets and antique shows, as
a 'picker' and as a 'hauler' and understands the
everyday workings of the antique trade.

Co-Author

Phil Dunning was born and educated in the
United States. He is Curator/Director of
Montgomery's Inn, an historic site in Toronto,
Ontario. He is the author of *The Canadiana
Guidebook: Antique Collecting in Ontario* and
of many articles in antiques magazines.
Prior to coming to Montgomery's Inn, he was
with the Canadiana Department of the
Royal Ontario Museum.
Phil lectures on antiques regularly and has
produced two series on antiques for television.
He has also been course director for several
seminars on furniture by the Ontario Museum
Association.

Designer/Producer

Catherine Thuro is a designer by profession.
Following study in the School of Architecture
at Auburn University, Alabama, she has
applied her considerable talents in such diverse
fields as architectural, landscape and interior
design, furniture, books and displays, and has
conducted her own landscape consulting
practice. She is the author/designer of
*Oil Lamps, the Kerosene Era in North America,
Primitives and Folk Art, our handmade heritage*
and the designer/producer of
The Marketplace Guide to Oak Furniture.
Catherine is also a well-known researcher,
lecturer, writer and consultant in the field of
early lighting.

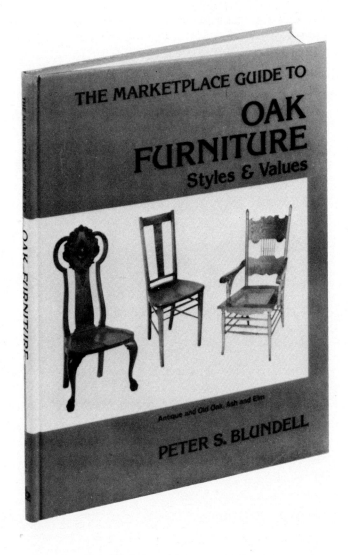